Giuseppe Sergi

The Varieties of the Human Species

Principles and method of classification

Giuseppe Sergi

The Varieties of the Human Species
Principles and method of classification

ISBN/EAN: 9783337370244

Printed in Europe, USA, Canada, Australia, Japan

Cover: Foto ©Andreas Hilbeck / pixelio.de

More available books at **www.hansebooks.com**

SMITHSONIAN MISCELLANEOUS COLLECTIONS

— 969 —

THE VARIETIES

OF THE

HUMAN SPECIES

PRINCIPLES AND METHOD

OF

CLASSIFICATION

BY

GIUSEPPE SERGI

Professor of Anthropology, Royal University of Rome, Italy

CITY OF WASHINGTON

PUBLISHED BY THE SMITHSONIAN INSTITUTION

1894

CONTENTS.

PART I.—BASIS OF HUMAN CLASSIFICATION.

PART II.—METHOD OF CLASSIFICATION.

I. THE VARIETIES.

II. THE SUBVARIETIES.

III. NOMENCLATURE.

A PREFATORY NOTE.

Doctor Giuseppe Sergi, professor of Anthropology in the Royal University of Rome, Italy, has made for himself a distinguished position by the ardor with which he has pursued the branch of science which he represents and the numerous valuable contributions he has made to its literature. A brief sketch of his career will form an appropriate introduction to the summary of his doctrines of craniology which is here translated.[1]

Dr. Sergi was born in Messina, Sicily, in 1841. His academic education was received in the Universities of Messina and Bologna, where he devoted himself especially to the departments of comparative anatomy and the philology of the Indo-European languages. In 1880 he was appointed to the chair of Anthropology in the University of Bologna, and four years later to the same position in the Faculty of Sciences of the University of Rome. In this field he has shown much energy, having by his personal exertions founded there the Museum of Anthropology and the Laboratory for Experimental Psychology. His lectures are attended by a constantly increasing class, and on the organization of the Society of Anthropology of Rome he was chosen as its first president, which position he still holds. He is also a regular, corresponding or honorary member of many learned societies in his own and other countries, among which may be mentioned in the United States the Anthropological Society of Washington, the American Philosophical Society, and the Numismatic and Antiquarian Society of Philadelphia.

His published works have been very numerous, beginning with " Principles of Psychology," in two volumes, issued at Messina in 1874, and of which a new edition is announced for this year (1894). These writings include a wide variety of subjects in physical and psychical anthropology and in education. Some are of a popular character, but the majority are strictly scientific and have been

---

[1] Le Varietà Umane. Principi e methodo di classificazione. Di Giuseppe Sergi. Torino, 1893. 8vo, pp. 60.

issued by learned societies and journals. Of especial note have
been his studies on the prehistoric peoples of the coasts of the
Mediterranean; on the native tribes of Melanesia; on human
degeneration and criminal anthropology; on the characteristics of
the female sex; and, in American subjects, on the physical anthropology of the Fuegians, on skulls of the Omaguas, on ancient
Peruvian skulls, and general considerations on American skulls.
His attention has been fruitfully attracted to the pigmy races
of Europe and to the varieties of the human species found in modern and ancient Russia, especially to the remains exhumed from
the "kourgans," or ancient sepulchral tumuli, which exist in
various districts of that state.

D. G. BRINTON.

THE VARIETIES OF THE HUMAN SPECIES.

PRINCIPLES AND METHOD OF CLASSIFICATION.

By Giuseppe Sergi.

PART FIRST.—Basis of Human Classification.

I.

In man, as in other animals, we find physical characteristics of two kinds, external and internal. The first are principally those pertaining to the cutis and certain cutaneous appendages, and include the coloring of the skin and hair, the structure and form of the hair, and also the coloring of the eyes. The chief internal characteristics are the bones from which the form and figure of all the members are taken, as well as those of the separate parts of the body clothed with soft tissues, such as muscles and fat. The cranium is the most important and most characteristic part of the entire human skeleton.

The cranium is a bony case which encloses a viscus of the first order, the brain, which in man is, in relation to the animal series, better developed, both in its forms and functions. It is known that the brain and cranium, from the embryological to the adult state, are in a parallel manner and gradually connected in evolution, and the external form of the one corresponds to that of the other. Most certainly it is not the cranium which gives form to the brain of man; It is more probable that it is the brain which moulds its organ of protection. Given hereditary conditions, we may affirm that the form of the cranium is correlative to that of the brain. If we could discover why the brain takes or has taken different forms we would possibly understand better its cores
pondence with the exterior structure of the cranium by which it is surrounded, though absolutely ignorant now. We might be

able to learn also what functional and especially what psychological characteristics are united to the cerebral forms which are revealed by cranial forms. All that is obscure for us, and also unexplored, because unsuspected; for in place of that, and in an inexact manner, the volume has been taken into account and therefore the weight of the brain, as being the only means of making an anthropological diagnosis of its functional value, the volume and weight corresponding to the capacity of the cranium.

But besides the cranium commonly called cerebral, there is the face, which, from the morphologic point of view, is not less important. The face has generally given more positive means for distinguishing human groups, not only on account of the coloring of the skin, but on account of the form and disposition of its parts, of the nose, of the cheeks, of the molar teeth, and on account of other characteristics which, when considered together, disclose differences not immediately revealed by the cerebral cranium.

The other parts of the skeleton also have differences more or less profound in the different ethnic groups, the stature, the length of the extremities, both absolutely and relatively to the stature and to the trunk; the thoracic form; and so on. But such differences seem little characteristic compared to those presented by the cranium and the face; until now, moreover, they have had but slight value, as should have those characteristics of classification which are merely secondary.

We are ignorant what may have been the primitive type or the primitive human types, considered in all their internal and external characteristics; that is, what skeletal forms certain ethnic groups of differently colored skin possessed; or, on the other hand, what color of skin and hair belonged to certain skeletal forms. That difficulty is caused by a fact easy to understand, by the mingling of different types among each other, and by the hybrid forms from which man is derived. It is true, however, that certain hybrid results seem to be limited to certain regions and to a few human groups; and that, on account of this, the elements which have furnished such products may be learned up to a certain point; but in the beginning, at least, it will be necessary to learn the structures of the parts from which hybrids are derived.

It is impossible not to admit human hybridism, since it is demonstrated clearly by all anthropologists; in this direction.

America alone shows us a perfect example of experimental anthropology. It is now determined from observations that human hybridism is multiform among all peoples; but what we learn from that example is the exchange of external characteristics and their mixture with those internal, that is, the union of the external characteristics of one ethnic type with the internal characteristics of another type. Thus, one may observe the color of the skin and hair with its special form united to characteristics of skeletons which do not generally belong to types of that color, and *vice versa*. That may be observed concerning certain characteristics, and not of all; such as the stature, or the face, with its soft covering, or the form of the cranium only.

If we study our European populations which are called white, but which have many gradations of whiteness, we may note the great mixture of characteristics, a mixture which is changeable, from which results a great variety of forms of individual types, constituted of characteristics differing from each other. An analysis must be very accurate and very minute to discriminate these different elements which exist in the composition of the ethnic characteristics of individuals and peoples. These mixtures and these combinations of characteristics differ according to the character and number of elements existing in the various nations of the south, the center, or the north of Europe. They arise from different relations with mixed peoples.

What is most important in this human hybridism, so various and so complex, is the lack of the blending of the external and internal characteristics from which new human varieties may be had. Among the different ethnic elements there exists only a relation of position, called syncretism, or propinquity of characteristics, and therefore a facility for forming small groups. Such a phenomenon has already been recognized in America, and it is evident in Europe among peoples who appear little homogeneous, if a careful observation separates the characteristics constituting ethnic types and those of individuals in a mixed population.

If there were no other cause for such an absence of blending among the characteristics of human hybridism, this cause would exist, that the relations which produce the mixtures are not equal and constant, but are varied and inconstant. If there should be the union of two pure ethnic types only, for several generations, we should be able to derive a hybrid product constant and fixed, as among animals and plants; but a third element, either pure or mixed, arrives in the second or third generation of man, and so on indefinitely. Thus it is easy to understand how unstable must be the characteristics of the hybrid, for they can scarcely survive in one individual for a generation. The hybrids which follow may have characteristics of different types, with the tendency each time to have these reappear by heredity, although not blended and not fixed in the individual.

To this should be added another fact, that of individual variation, which is present in man, as in other animals, increased by his constant interminglings, which may be considered stimulants of this phenomenon, as has been suggested by Darwin and Wallace.

Hence, I conclude from my observations, that human hybridism is a syncretism of characteristics belonging to many varieties, and that these do not modify the skeletal forms as do individual variations, and that hybridism may affect different parts of the skeleton, constituting characteristics in themselves distinct. The stature, the thoracic form, the proportion of the long bones, may be united with external characteristics differing from each other, as well as from different cranial structures. The cranial form may be associated with different facial forms, and inversely. It happens, however, that the structures taken separately remain in part unvaried in the hybrid constitution. The face preserves its own characteristics in spite of the union of different cranial forms; so also the cranium preserves its structures, associating them with different facial forms. The stature preserves its own proportions in spite of its association with different cranial and facial types, and in spite of the different coloration of the skin and the form and color of the hair. All this may be affirmed, particularly of much larger human groups which, according to external characteristics, may be considered much nearer than they really are in geographical position, as the so-called white races in Europe, the negroes in Africa, in Melanesia, and so on.

Now, granting that all peoples exhibit the characteristics of hybridism in the manner just described, it will be necessary to learn how races, groups and human families may be classified. Let us observe for a moment the classification by means of external characteristics, most common among anthropologists from Linnaeus to Quatrefages and Flower, and we shall see:

1). That the color of the human skin in one great group of a type, such as yellow, black, or white, is of different gradations and not uniform.

2). Since, as above stated, all peoples, at least in a great measure, are composed of hybrid elements, it happens that different elements are united under one category, which is, in this instance, the color of the skin.

3). We must not forget that the external characteristics are more easily lost, and much easier to acquire, by intermixture and heredity.

A curious example of what I state is found in human classification according to Quatrefages, which perhaps is now the most complete, considered only as a classification by external characteristics. He places the Abyssinians within the white race notwithstanding that they have the negro coloring, and he does so because he believes that the characteristic form of the skeleton or internal characteristics of the Abyssinians are those of the white race. This is without doubt inconsistent when the principle of classification by color is accepted. This inconsistency itself shows the defect of the method and of the principles mentioned as applied to human characteristics and their combination.

4). Finally, as we perceive, the theory is not justified that man be classified as a single species with three, five or more variations.

If the characteristics which present greater stability are internal or skeletal, they should serve for human classification:

1st. Because, notwithstanding amalgamation and consequent hybridism, the characteristics originating in the skeleton are persistent.

2d. Because they may be taken as fixed points with which other characteristics may be associated, and may be also external, as I shall demonstrate.

3d. Because, finally, the internal characteristics can demonstrate the full number of divisions and subdivisions in classifying ethnic groups, and in analyzing peoples which are a combination of a great number of hybrids.

It remains to determine which internal characteristics should have the preference in deciding the value of types for classification. If we consider the human skeleton, with that object in view, we find three parts which may serve for that purpose, the cerebral cranium, the face, and the stature, with the long bones.

Stature.—The stature is a good, but an insufficient characteristic, because it gives only linear differences, and in its value resembles greatly other external characteristics, and is associated with all the most dissimilar derived from the skeleton.

Face.—The face offers very important characteristics for classi-fication, because it shows typical differences in the ethnic groups. The face has given more points for the distinction of human types than the other parts of the human body, and would appear better adapted for that purpose than the cerebral cranium. But the face is more disposed to individual variations than any other part, because it is very complex, being composed of numerous small bones, clothed with muscles which have continuous and important functions relating to the physiognomy, to the expression of psychi-cal conditions, and to the nutritive functions. These facts render its typical form less constant, and are, or may be, the cause of a multiplication of types.

Cranium.—The cerebral cranium is itself also liable to varia-tions. More than any other organ, it exhibits a phenomenon often observed and clearly demonstrated by me, that is, the per-sistence of forms from immemorial epochs, and their reproduction through numerous generations notwithstanding amalgamation with other types. I have demonstrated such a persistence of cranial forms in the varieties of the Mediterranean from the Neo-lithic and from the most ancient Egyptian epochs; other anthro-pologists have recognized such persistence in European types of the Quaternary epoch, and in others, very ancient, from America. This cannot be said of the structure of the face.

Therefore if the human cranium is accepted as the basis for the classification of human groups, positive results may be had:

1st. In groups which have been subjected to mixture in what-ever epoch or however many times, the distinctive ethnic elements may be discerned by examining the cerebral cranium only, which, remaining unaltered in type, may be found united by hybridism with other internal and external characteristics. For the cranium is the point about which revolve all other variations of form, either in hybridism or in the human form itself.

2d. Knowing the cranial types of a people who seem more or less homogeneous, we are sure of learning of what and how many ethnic elements it is composed, notwithstanding the hybridism present.

3d. Having classified all the cranial types in different regions and among different peoples, we may learn by their geographical distribution the numerical extension of types and also their geographical origin; that is, the place of departure and the course of emigration and dispersion of such forms.

4th. Then it will be easy to learn what cranial characteristics are found among populations which already have ethnic names, ancient and modern, and to discover among them points of similarity and difference.

Being, therefore, obliged on acount of universal human hybridism to select as a guide to classification the most important and the most useful of the internal characteristics, we find greater advantages in choosing the human cranium, about which all the other characteristics, internal and external, are grouped. If we select one characteristic, or a number of variable characteristics, we shall find ourselves in the same position as other anthropologists who classify by external or accessory traits. It follows that accepting the cranium as the principal internal characteristic, we impliedly accept the brain in its various forms, and the brain is the most important of human organs.

II.

The classification of man by means of the cranium alone is by no means new. It will be well to consider these schemes, from that of Retzius down to the last, that of Kollmann. Nor, indeed, is the conception of the importance and superiority of the cranium for distinguishing ethnic groups by any means recent. To show that, we have but to refer to the enormous work which has been done, from Morton to Davis and Thurman, from Broca to G. Retzius, to De Quatrefages, to von Holder, to Ecker, to His and Rutimeyer, to Virchow, to Ranke, to others still more numerous, in Italy, from Nicolucci to Mantegazza.

Notwithstanding so much labor expended on the human cranium, satisfactory results were not reached, nor, indeed, I may affirm, have we yet reached them, at least not in the signification which I intend these results to have. The fault lies in the nature of the method of studying the human cranium and in the value attributed to craniometry.

The classification of Retzius is based upon a single characteristic of the cranium, which, however, is merely the numerical expression of the *norma verticalis* of Blumenbach, that is, the cephalic index.

According to Retzius we have only two forms of crania, the long and short; though, in fact, many forms of short and long crania are found differing very much from each other.

When craniometry was developed in a systematic manner, following principally the work of Broca, it appeared the key of anthropology, and took the first place among means of investigations, as being the most effectual method for distinguishing human races. The French exaggerated its value; the Italians followed with zeal, in spite of the skepticism of Mantegazza, the head of the Florentine school of anthropology; the Germans have been more rational, and with them the Swiss, represented by His and Rutimeyer. At the head of them I would place Blumenbach, who based his small but valuable book upon a rational foundation.[1] The Germans try to establish cranial type almost or entirely independent of the cephalic index; as one may see from the works of von Holder, of Ecker, of His and Rutimeyer, of Virchow, of Kollmann, of Ranke and others. In my opinion the German method is an approximation to the truth, but unfortunately the conception of type is undeveloped and, I should say, has remained rudimental, because craniometry, like a pernicious weed among the grain, injures the harvest. Virchow, the most pronounced scholar in anthropology, and the man who has studied more than all others the crania of all peoples, believes that the germ of a sound anthropology should develop from it. He concedes only a secondary value to craniometry; but, nevertheless, in his last work, *precisely when he distinguishes types*, attempting to establish them definitely, he determines them by craniometry alone. In fact, in his great work, *Crania Ethnica Americana*, he defines types in this manner: " Die Form ist long, schmal und relativ hoch," or, " Die Form des Schädels ist hypsi-brachycephal," and gives the index and the measures. Now the reader who will observe that the Araucanians, the Pampeans, the Chilians of Huanilla and of Copiapo, and the Peruvians of Iquique, have the

---

[1] *De generis humani varietate nativa.* IIIa edit. Göttingen, 1795.

hypsi-brachycephalic form of cranium, will not understand why the illustrious author constitutes of them different types, defining them always with the often-repeated proposition, " Die Form des Schädels ist hypsi-brachycephal." That the forms of such crania differ is evident from the fine lithographs, and not from the description, much less from the definition. Why has the celebrated anthropologist stopped on the way and has not developed the idea already promulgated by him and by his compatriots? I find in the *Crania Helvetica* and in the *Crania Germanica* of von Holder and of Ecker that the conception of type is more evident and has also a nomenclature, which is the only means of distinguishing typical forms.

According to my observations upon craniometry, which has now become cabalistic, especially in France, on account of the abuse of measures and numerical ciphers, the indices of the cranium and face are taken as a means of distinguishing races, human groups, as we might call them, and other measures are either omitted or applied only to individuals. In order to be convinced we should carefully and conscientiously study the craniometrical works of Dr. Danielli, of Florence, upon the Nias and Bengalese. The author has not been able to find satisfactory results after persevering researches, but whoever would seek evidence of individual variations will find more than enough. It seems to me, therefore, that the method by measurement may serve this purpose, that is, to discover numerically individual differences, but never those typical of a race. But such a discovery is useless, since we are all convinced of the existence of individual differences. I will therefore add that such differences, to be valuable, must be sought, not among forms differing from each other, but among individuals of the same type. That implies, therefore, necessarily and always, the search for types and their distinction, which is not possible by means of the craniometrical method.

Craniometry considers two forms, with a third of transition : the cranium long, and relatively narrow; the cranium wide, and relatively short, that is, dolicho- and brachycephalic, the form between which is mesocephalic. These forms, as I have said, are expressions of the normal line of Blumenbach, but imperfect, inexact and insufficient, as a brief demonstration will show.

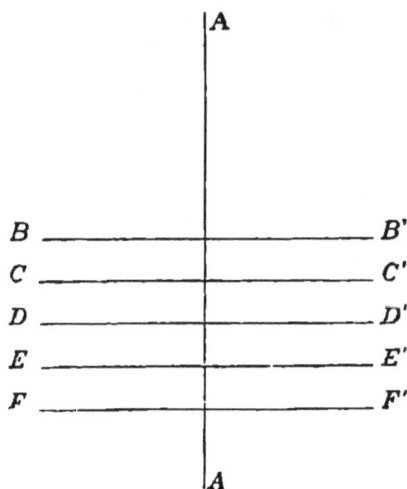

FIG. 1.

Let AA' be the antero-posterior diameter of a cranium, BB' the greatest transverse; it is evident that, given the norma verticalis with such diameters and with the greatest transverse at the conjunction of the line BB', this norma verticalis takes a particular form on account of the curves which surround the two diameters. This line or curve, which surrounds them, is called X. If the greatest transverse is placed back and is made to coincide with the line CC', the curve will be modified and will no longer be X but Y. That will be equally true if the transverse diameter is placed still further back at DD', EE', FF'; then we shall have a third curve Z, a fourth, a fifth, n, that is, we shall have as many different vertical curves on account of the changing of the diameter of the width, as the index causes ; that is, the relation between the length and the width will be the same.

From this it may be judged how much more will the norma verticalis vary if the form of the curve circumscribing the two diameters be modified in other ways, that is, by the frontal width, by the occipital form, and so on. If we also add the lateral curves, those posterior and anterior, which serve to show the form of this irregular body, we shall easily be convinced that the cephalic and vertical index cannot give the cranial form. That is why I have above stated that the expression of Virchow, " The form of the cranium is hypsi-brachycephalic," is insufficient to define the form. While cranial types so defined have equal indices, their curves differ in degree, and therefore the skull may or not be hypsi-brachycephalic. It is just as if we attempt to calculate the size of an ellipsis by means of the relation of its two axes. Two ellipses equal in this relation may be unequal in size, and this is why these two relations cannot be compared. It is the same in regard to the cephalic and vertical indices of the cranium.

If it were true and there were no doubt respecting the value of the celebrated cephalic index in determining cranial forms, it would follow that all human crania of whatever type and volume should be placed in the three categories of dolicho-, meso-, and brachycephalic, or of hypsi-, ortho-, and chamaecephalic. Thus all the populations of the earth, either of white, yellow, black or red skin, would have crania belonging to the three categories. A classification solely according to the cephalic index is therefore an absurdity. It is incoherent and without meaning, as are those of Retzius and Kollmann.

This conclusion is so true that such anthropologists are obliged to add descriptions to the forms of each part of the cranium, in order to distinguish it, recognizing the insufficiency of cranial data. Such descriptions can, to a certain degree only, supply the defect of the method, but they always remain incomplete, and leave the forms or types of the human cranium of various populations and regions indefinite. The French school has gone still farther and has supplied the deficiency with an infinite number of measurements, which only increase the obscurity, leaving the conception of the form more uncertain, and fatiguing the most patient student, who becomes convinced of never reaching any satisfactory result from such a confused accumulation of numbers.

In order to render classification more definite, or for the sake of finding a second characteristic which might be associated with the cephalic index, Retzius turned his attention to the prognathism and the orthognathism of the molar teeth; Kollmann to the facial index. Use could be made of the nasal index instead of the facial, or the orbital index, or any isolated characteristic, and we should have the same results. The combinations given by Retzius and Kollmann are possible, but cannot indicate races or varieties, from the fact that they are hybrid associations.

I need not make a longer demonstration of what I have affirmed, that classifications of human groups have been attempted by means of the cerebral cranium, but have not been successful on account of deficiency of method; and that the craniometrical method, still so undeveloped, has not yet, nor cannot, give those results while there is an exaggeration of an exact principle, that of expressing numerically facts relating to the cranium. It seems to me, after several years of study, and after having adopted the accepted form of craniometry, for want of a better, that it is time to establish for our use and for the study of the variations of man, a natural method, resembling that which is used in zoology and botany, and of which I laid the foundation about two years ago.

III.

The human cranium presents two kinds of variations: the first are those which change their general form and present types differing from each other; the second are those which do not change their typical form. The first have stable characteristics, therefore hereditary, and which passing through many generations remain unaltered and persistent; the second are the variations of the individuals of a type, and, of course, being transitory, do not in any way alter the typical forms; they are the so-called "individual" variations.

There is no need of recapitulating the facts which relate to variations in the human cranium, nor of seeking their causes, since the investigations of Darwin, Wallace and others concerning the variability of organisms, well known to all students of biology. I would simply state that the various phenomena of variation are repeated in man, and, for the case in point, in the human cranium.

The relation which exists between the two kinds of variations is close, and it is possible to admit that individual variations have given origin to permanent variations, just as it is easy to accept the idea that the process of variation in animals and in man in the cranium and the brain is continuous and constant. However that may be, an observer accustomed to large and small series of human heads perceives immediately that such series may be divided into groups, different and distinct, according to the form of the cranium itself, and that some difference, often difficult to describe or explain, exists among the elements of the groups; and this difference is derived precisely from the individual variations of the groups themselves. While the character of individual variations is transitory, the character of those which give typical forms is permanent; their persistence consists in being hereditary and numerous in each generation.

We know that the so-called " species " of the animal kingdom have forms derived from some variations of characteristics, and that they are such because the variations from the mother-species are permanent and become transmitted by heredity. These forms may be called " varieties " of the " species," or races, according to some, or subspecies, according to others. We will call them " varieties," because the name indicates their immediate origin. According to Darwin, a variety is a species in the process of formation, because it still bears many characteristics of the species from which it is derived, and cannot become an independent form, like the species itself, until it acquires still more diverging characteristics.

If we apply this principle to the human cranium, we should first learn if man comprises a single species, as many anthropologists believe, or has many species. In the first case, the typical variations of the cranium would certainly be varieties; if, however, there are several human species, the problem becomes more complicated. In that case the varieties might be of one species, and a primitive type be found to which it is allied. But if of such primitive types there were several, these would form several species which should be grouped under one genus.

I cannot venture the solution of the general question regarding the unity or plurality of the human species, considering the actual state of my personal observations, limited to Southern Europe, especially the Mediterranean, to Oriental Europe, and to the Kourgans of Russia. I should examine Asia, Africa, Oceanica, America, Central and Northern Europe, before being able to give an opinion on such a problem. I will call therefore varieties only, human varieties, the typical forms of the cranium which are clearly distinguished from each other by their own and diverging characteristics, while I will suppose that such varieties may converge in different species, of which I cannot now give the type nor characteristics.   Meanwhile it is useful to know and describe the "varieties" under this name, with the purpose of learning their distribution in the various regions of the earth.

With the present uncertainty about human varieties, I could have no intention of publishing a work which would treat of general theories, nor would I have thought of the present pamphlet had not necessity demanded it.   This essay is only designed to give direction to the method of research, because many students have requested it, and in order to place before the public ideas and facts which others either misunderstand or condemn without knowing them.

Calling the typical forms of the cranium "varieties," we have the advantage of finding the differences or individual variations of the same type, and also certain differences which cannot be reduced to individual variations, but which are equally repeated as diverging characteristics of the same variety: these constitute subordinate groups or "subvarieties."   The "subvariety" therefore diverges from the "variety" by a new characteristic which it retains in a persistent manner.   We have an easy means of recognizing varieties and subvarieties, and of distinguishing them from individual variations.   The latter are not repeated, or if there is repetition it is accidental; varieties are repeated by groups more or less large, which, in addition, have individual variations; the subvarieties also repeat in lesser groups that characteristic or those characteristics of the variety from which they are derived.

One of the difficulties of craniologists is how to find the limits of individual variations, how to distinguish them from typical forms, or to admit that all cranial variations may be individual, especially if one population is studied without reflecting that any population is invariably a composition of many varieties, notwithstanding the misleading appearance of the external form and the exterior characteristics.   We can clearly and easily distinguish by my method the individual variations from the true and constant varieties and from the subvarieties, and we can make a complete analysis of populations, as I have had numerous occasions to demonstrate.

Another prejudice of anthropologists is that human varieties, determined by my method, may be too numerous.   The scientist cannot, indeed, free himself of certain sentiments which are acquired in following scientific habits and which have become a part of science and public opinion, because in face of the danger of seeing human varieties doubled or decupled, he feels an aversion, like an instinct of preservation for that which is established and which has become the belief of most scientists and cultivated men. The human races until now have been either three, four or five, but never six; the first time it is affirmed that they may be twenty, opposition is inevitable; it is the *misoneism* of Lombroso, the inertia of the mind, which opposes such resistance, just as matter is opposed to every change in the direction of its forces. Treating of man, into which we ourselves enter with our sentiments, the opposition is greater, even in spite of good intentions. Notwithstanding this psychological phenomenon which influences us all, the force of facts is superior to every inertia and sooner or later will conquer.

With the observations and the methods which I propose, I believe that many errors will be eliminated from anthropology. Those errors have been accepted because we have never possessed natural scientific methods for the study of human classification, such as we have in zoology. To apply zoological methods to man appeared to lower him to his congenerous beings; and, while in zoology, science advances freely, in anthropology, on the other hand, preoccupations embarrass researches. I observe that such preoccupations do not exist in two very eminent anthropologists, although the contrary at first appears evident in one of them—Blumenbach and De Quatrefages—at least a century apart. Blumenbach, in a valuable little book, attempts to apply the zoological method to man, not only for classification, but for the explanation of the causes of animal and human varieties. De Quatrefages, in his last work, employs the same method and the same scientific freedom. Unfortunately the followers or successors of both have only followed their masters in form, but not in method. Blumenbach, who, after various researches, reduces the human species to five varieties, finds, however, that human variations are infinite in number. If his method had been followed strictly, the number of human varieties would long ago have been increased, both in respect to the structure and the cranial forms.

The neglect of such methods and the failure to distinguish human varieties by means of the cranium has caused a curious error, that of regarding certain forms which are typically normal, as pathological, as I shall have occasion to demonstrate in the future when I speak of classified forms. This is apt to happen when new and unrecognized forms are placed before the observer.

One of the important characteristics in classifying the cranial varieties of man is the *cranial capacity,* which has a direct relation to the volume and weight of the brain; hence classification by crania means the classification of brains estimated by their form and external configuration. Its importance is for us increased by the fact that that which we find among races of animals occurs also in man; that there are races of small and large animals, races differing in size. This is also repeated in man, and we therefore have large, medium and small varieties, as measured by stature. The origin of such varieties is perfectly analogous to that in other animals. Nor is it an accidental phenomenon, because it is confirmed by heredity, through numerous and indefinite generations.

I have concluded, in studying cranial varieties morphologically as human varieties, that is, by their characteristic structures, that the volume has a direct relation to the form, that is, many forms have limited and definite capacities, while other forms have subvarieties differing in capacity. Such varieties are analogous to the stature of the large and small varieties of animals. The cranial capacity, therefore, while it is one of the integral characteristics of the cranium in regard to its classification, is also the indication of different varieties according to size. I discovered this fact when I classified for the first time the crania of Melanesia, and subsequently I defined it more accurately when I examined and classified thousands of other human crania.

This fact points to a correction of the value of cranial capacity and therefore of the weight of the brain, until now calculated by the average without distinction among different varieties. The cranial capacity of man varies from 1000 cc. to about 2000 cc. in the masculine sex; this enormous difference is admitted as individual variation, and it is thus conceded that there may be a least limit of normality possible which can be ascribed to the function of the brain, crania which descend to 1150 cc. being considered as pathological microcephali, according to Broca, and more or less according to other anthropologists; giving, on the other hand, a great value to a large capacity. Both conclusions are contrary to the real significance of the facts. I have found normal masculine capacities of 1000 cc. and a little greater, representing small human varieties, not being sporadic and individual phenomena; and, on the other hand, anthropologists have registered for eminent men like Dante, Gauss and others, very mediocre capacities, even very low, while for ordinary men they have recorded a much higher capacity. I have found in Melanesia normally constituted heads absolutely microcephalic, together with megalocephalic heads, belonging to varieties which have the same social value; they are both inferior, some anthropophagous, and live mixed together as one people. That which I have asserted concerning Melanesia may be said of the ancient and modern populations of the Mediterranean, among which are the Sicilians, the Sardinians, and the inhabitants of Central and Southern Italy; and I do not believe it can be said that there are no signs of human superiority in those regions. There are not, therefore, individual differences so great' as from 1000 to 1500 cc., and from 1500 to 2000 cc., but characteristic differences of variety in human forms. The general average I therefore maintain is inexact and still further arbitrary, because it is the average of incommensurate quantities. The exact average is that between individuals of the same variety, and the difference is the true individual variation.

But there is another error to correct due to the signification which I am able to give to varieties distinguished by means of my method. It is considered by some a demonstrated fact that the cranial capacity has been increased in the course of social evolution from prehistoric epochs to historic times. Eminent men have affirmed it, but I have already placed their conclusions in doubt, because the facts do not appear to me evident and affirmative. I wrote some years ago:[1] "The most important physical evolution of man would be that which related to the organ of the mental functions, the brain. But the facts are still very doubtful and very obscure which relate to the weight and volume of the brain, and consequently to the cranial capacity. In a recent work of Professor Schmidt I find that the cranial capacity of the ancient pure Egyptians is 1394 cc. in the masculine and 1257 in the feminine sex; in the pure modern Egyptians it is 1421 in the males, 1206 in

---

[1] *Human Evolution.* Review of Scientific Philosophy, 1888, Milan.

the females. According to these figures there would be an increase of the cranial capacity of the modern over the ancient males, but a decrease in the females. The reverse would be true of the Egypto-Nubian cranium, which is 1335 in the modern males and 1205.8 in the females. Broca found that the Egyptians of the IV. Dynasty had, males 1534, females 1397 cc.; those of the XI., males 1443, females 1328; and, finally, those of the XXIII., the most recent, males 1464, females 1322. There would be in such a case no increase, but decrease, but that is not possible; the cause of these facts lies in the mixtures of races at different times and in different proportions."

Now I conclude from my recent studies upon the Egyptians of different dynasties, from the most ancient to the present, that according to my method of classification there are capacities of 1260 cc., of 1390, of 1480, of 1550, of 1710, and still other capacities differing according to the varieties determined.[1] As is easily understood, a general average necessarily alters the facts, according to the number of varieties which enter as components of the average in the different series in anthropological museums; hence the curious results above indicated.

Another important point is as follows:

" But the fact which surprises us is the high figure of the capacity given by prehistoric crania. The masculine crania of Lozère have given 1606 cc., the feminine 1507; also of Lozère, masculine 1578, feminine 1473; crania from the *pietra levigata*, masculine 1531, feminine 1320; the contemporaneous Parisians, masculine 1559, feminine 1337. The approximate average of crania from the *pietra levigata* is 1560, equal to that of modern Europeans, as is related by Topinard."[2]

In another of my recent works I have demonstrated that of the crania of the neolithic age[3] the *Isobathyplatycephalus* has a capacity from 1230 to 1405 in the feminine, and the *Eucampylos* varies from 1470 to 1564 in the masculine. The two varieties, still persistent in Sicily, do not vary in capacity in the modern series, and at the same time show that in the neolithic epochs, as among

---

[1] *Concerning the Primitive Inhabitants of the Mediterranean*, Archives of Anthropology, Florence, 1892, Vol. XXII.

[2] See *Human Evolution*.

[3] *Crania of the Neolithic Age*, Boll. Paletnol. Italiana, Parma, 1892.

modern populations, large and small varieties are found, just as the same types are now found through persistence of forms.

From this it is evident how much there is to reform in anthropology when we study by natural methods facts until the present misinterpreted, respecting the classification as well as the physical and psychological characteristics of man in time and space. Perhaps in the future, when we know all cranial forms by natural classification, it will be possible to find a correspondence of psychological characteristics in populations according to the predominance or superiority of types, a fact which has until now escaped research, because the capacity of the cranium in its absolute sense is not in correlation to the development of the mental functions, notwithstanding what is commonly affirmed. The reform is urgent, but a natural method should be employed, and that is my purpose.

PART SECOND.—Method and Classification.

I.

Varieties.

The greatest variation in a series of human crania cannot be distinguished by an untrained eye; anatomists continually accustomed to the study of the human skeleton and scholastic demonstrations do not at first discover the salient points of difference among crania, their attention being distracted by observing the single parts of which they are composed, the canals, depressions and minor details, and does not grasp the complex form of the entire cranium. There are two different kinds of observations: one is useful in examining the development and normal condition of the cranium; the other serves for the classification of forms, and it is this last method of inquiry which I am about to consider.

The distinctions of forms depend in the first place on the comparison of different crania. They should be placed upon a table and compared in every direction. Little by little a useful habit and keen eye are acquired, by means of which the slightest variations are detected, so that the similarity of fundamental characteristics can be seen among great differences which at first appear absolutely dissimilar.

The practical method which I have already adopted, for me and others who wish to make use of it, is that of placing the series of crania in order and in an equal row upon a large table, the first time, if possible, of the same color, intact, that is, without having been sawed to extract the brain, without the lower jaw, and therefore upon a single plane, each placed upon its base. Difference of color, the line which divides a cranium sawed, an inequality in the table, may alter the positions of the forms or render the discovery of similarities and differences more difficult.

When familiarity with the forms has once been acquired, many of the conditions become superfluous, and then an isolated cranium is classified without the necessity of a comparison, at least in the forms which are common.

After various and attentive observations and continuous comparisons, it is necessary to form groups of crania which seem to have common characteristics. Formed in groups, each group must be separately analyzed in every component, in order to recognize common and diverging characteristics; if these last are marked, separate the groups into subgroups, noting the individual differences which must necessarily exist.

Formed in groups and subgroups, one typical cranium is selected for each group or subgroup, and its likeness is transferred by drawing a free-hand outline, by placing the cranium itself upon paper, or by means of a camera, and finally the volume is reduced, or rather the linear magnitude, to a third or half, making this reduction equal in all the crania which are designed. Drawing has the very great advantage of revealing the linear curves, which are not immediately observed, and demonstrates characteristic differences very easily. In case of doubt concerning certain forms which seem similar, it is well to place the profiles one above another, in order readily to observe similarities and differences, whether apparent or real, profound or superficial.

The following are additional rules: Distinguish the crania which compose the groups according to sex, because sexual differences should not impair or alter the types under which the crania are classed, nor should another type be made on account of characteristics which are merely sexual. The observer should be trained to discover the sexes of crania and sexual characteristics distinctly and clearly. When the groups are formed, the crania should be adult, though when special conditions permit, those of infants can be added. We should bear in mind that the forms of the latter are never decided, just as they are not permanent. The condition of the sutures and of normal or abnormal development should be taken into account, because abnormal development, as well as the partial arrest of development, may profoundly alter typical forms; exclude, therefore, all pathological crania when this pathological condition is apparent. I have, however, been able to observe and will demonstrate in a future work[1] that crania belonging to persons of enfeebled mind, in spite of various alterations, preserve the typical forms and are recognizable without difficulty by those experienced in the method and classes of forms.

The examination of the cranium must begin with the well-known *norma verticalis* of Blumenbach, that *norma* from which, in turn, Retzius derives the index of the width. It should furnish us the first form or the first characteristic for classification. When the vertical line is undecided, or cannot be reduced to a normal form, then the norma lateralis must be observed in order to ascertain the first characteristic; it may also happen that the lateral modifies the norma verticalis so profoundly that it may be preferred to this, or that it may have a characteristic much more prominent and more easily distinguished than the vertical; in such a case it should have the first place. It may also happen that another characteristic may be more decided and more marked, giving it the preference, and such a characteristic may be visible in the norma occipitalis or norma facialis; this should then be selected as the first characteristic for distinguishing varieties.

Let us now consider those characteristics which should separate and classify varieties according to the natural method. I begin with the forms given by the *norma verticalis*, as they are those which are easily distinguished and can be in great part reduced to geometrical figures.

1st. ELLIPSOID (*ellipsoides*) (Fig. 2).

We will call *ellipsoid* a cranium which in the norma verticalis presents an elliptical contour, as in the figure reproduced, taken from life, and which I insert in the parallelogram in order to show

---

[1] This is the work of Dr. G. Mingazzini, entitled *Concerning the Craniology of the Insane.*

its regularity and demonstrate how the exterior outline harmonizes with the lines which surround it. Ellipsoid, or whatever similar name is adopted, signifies a body which has an outline similar to an ellipsis. Such an elliptical form, very common among varieties of crania, necessarily has all the projections rounded off, the occipital is never flat, and the parietal protuberances are always slight, or do not exist; the transverse curve of the norma verticalis or cranial arch is moderately or decidedly convex.

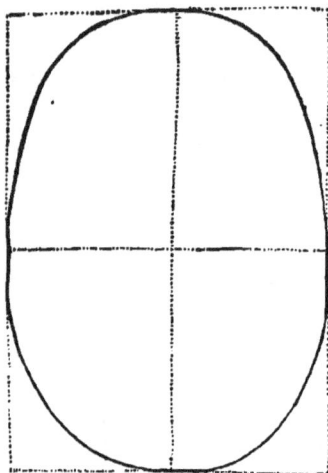

Fig. 2.—Ellipsoides.

A form of this kind, considered only as norma verticalis, is subject to variations in length and width; hence it may be a short and wide ellipsis, *brachyellipsoid* (*brachyellipsoides*), a long one or a narrow one, *dolichellipsoid* or *stenellipsoid*.

2d. Pentagonoid (*pentagonoides*) (Fig. 3).

Figure 3 shows a pentagon of unequal sides, but symmetrical, into which is inserted a cranial form corresponding to its respective sides, but with rounded angles, of which the most rounded, which is cut off, is that which corresponds to the occipital cone. In this cranial type the parietal protuberances are pointed, and often with corners definite and acute; from these points towards the frontal there is a gradual narrowing, and so also towards the occipital; but with this difference, that while from the parietal protuberances forward this narrowing, which forms the two symmetrical sides, is maintained almost at the same level as the cranial arch, the level from the parietal protuberances to the occiput becomes oblique and descends to form the angle of the pentagon.

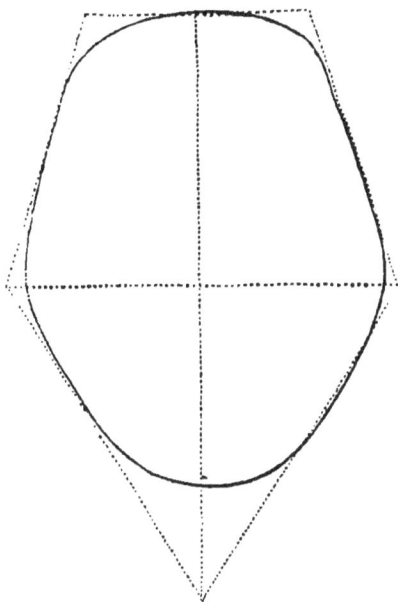

FIG. 3.—PENTAGONOIDES.

This obliquity is very evident when seen from the norma verticalis (Fig. 4).

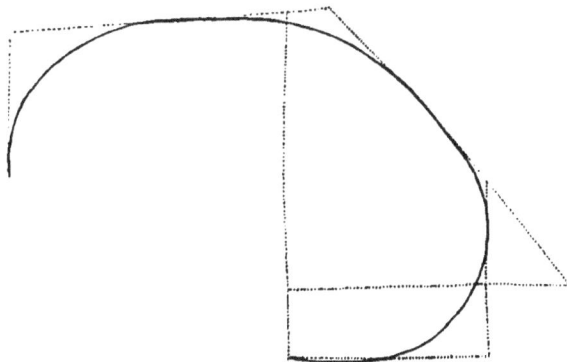

FIG. 4.—PENTAGONOIDES.

The variations which the pentagonal norma verticalis may present are as follows:

1st. The corners are acute or obtuse; whence a *pentagonoides acutus* and *obtusus :* the anterior part of the cranium, that is, the two sides which reunite the parietal to the frontal protuberances, can be longer or shorter than usual; there will then be a *pentagonoides oblongus* or a *brachypentagonoides.*

3d. RHOMBOID (*rhomboides*).

The rhomboidal form of the norma verticalis (Fig. 5) can interchange with the pentagonal form, because the most characteristic difference consists in the suppression of the one side corresponding to the frontal width.

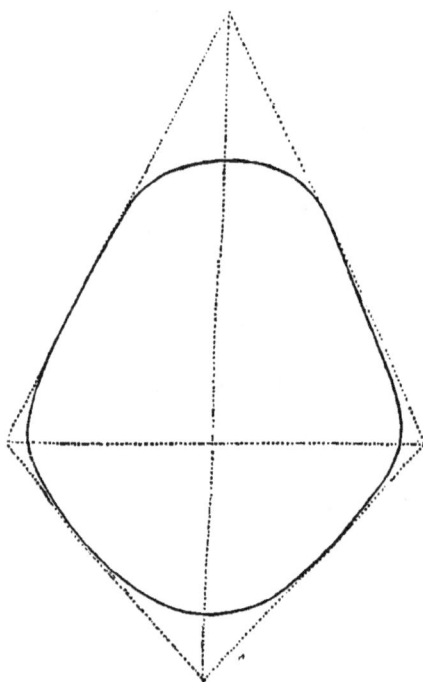

FIG. 5.—RHOMBOIDES.

This side is very short in the rhomboidal figure of the cranium when considered in relation to the biparietal width of which the protuberances are very distinct and pointed; so the occipital projection is still more acute on account of the greater convergence of the two posterior sides. In this variety the cranium is smooth in the sagittal line, low in relation to its width and length.

Of this singular form I have so far found two variations distinguishable by the norma verticalis: 1st, the *australensis*, of which I give the type in Fig. 5; and 2d, the *brachyrhomboides aegyptiacus*, shorter and wider than the preceding.

N. B. That these forms are often found in infantile crania is a fact worthy of attention.

4th. OVOID (*ovoides*).   This form (Fig. 6) is distinguishable only by the norma verticalis.   The enlargement of the cranium is at the parietals at about a third of their entire length and posteriorly. The occiput terminates at the large apex of the egg, while the second apex is represented by the frontal.   The cranium has symmetrical curves; the arch is not always very convex and may have a transverse curve, slight and easy.

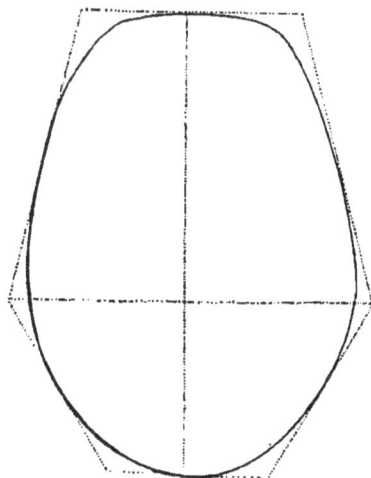

FIG. 6.—OVOIDES.

The ovoid cannot be confused with the pentagonoid, because it has no sides, nor apparent corners, nor has it the occipital obliquity which forms the posterior part of the two posterior sides of the pentagonoid.

The "Sardinian ovoid," which I have described and named *sardiniensis*, diverges a little from this type; the enlargement of the parietals is situated a little in advance of that in the type described, and, besides, the ovoidal appearance is also perceived in the norma lateralis.

5th. SPHENOID (*sphenoides*).

The cranium represented in Fig. 7, which I name " sphenoid,"
from the Greek, is cuneiform.   The characteristics of this type are

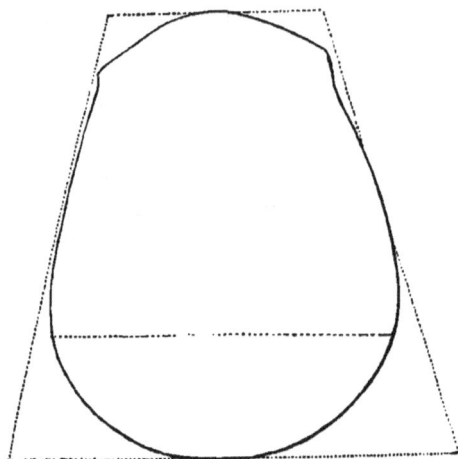

FIG. 7.—SPHENOIDES.

very evident; the biparietal enlargement of the cranium is far back,
and there is a gradual and sensible reduction in width from that

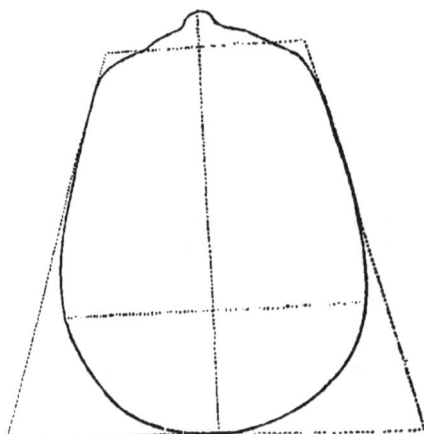

FIG. 8.—SPHENOIDES STENOMETROPUS.

unusually large extension as far as the frontal.   The occipital
part is, therefore, either level and vertical, or rounded, without protuberance.

This form, seen in the norma verticalis only, is subject to many variations, preserving, however, the characteristics which clearly distinguish it from others. I add some of the most common forms which I have found and classified.

1. *Sphenoides stenometropus*, that with a narrow forehead and generally a small capacity. This type is very common in the Mediterranean (Fig. 8).

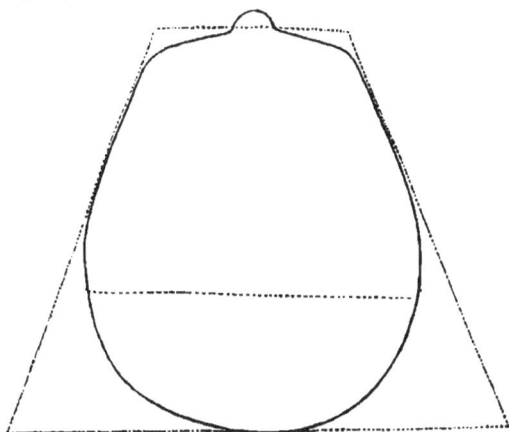

FIG. 9.—SPHENOIDES ROTUNDUS.

2. *Sphenoides rotundus* (Fig. 9), which is larger and wider than

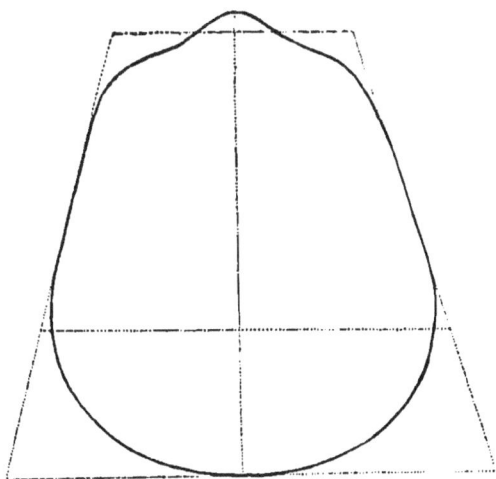

FIG. 10.—SPHENOIDES LATUS.

the former, and has the elevations rounded off, especially in the occipital part, which is globular.

3. *Sphenoides latus* (Fig. 10). This is much wider in its biparietal expansion and is short. It has the occipital smooth and per-

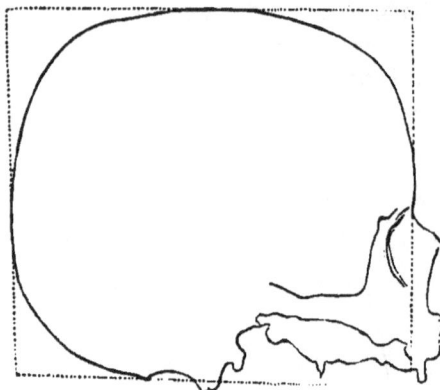

FIG. 11.—SPHENOIDES LATUS.

pendicular, the parietal prominences acute, the corners evident and the sides flat; observed laterally, this type appears cuboid (Fig. 11).

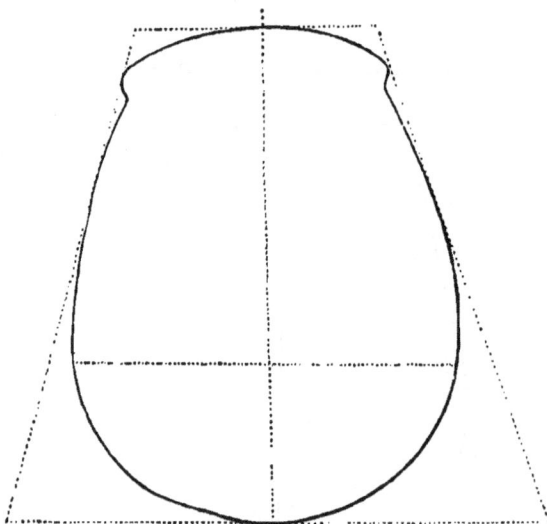

FIG. 12.—SPHENOIDES MEGAS.

This is the characteristic type of the Kourgans of Russia, and for that reason I have called it *kurganicus*.

4. *Sphenoides megas* (Fig. 12), the largest which I have found. It is also distinguished in the norma verticalis by a certain convexity in the sides of the cranium and by the posterior rotundity. This type is also obtained from the Kourgans.

5. *Sphenoides oblongus.* I so name that sphenoid which has a marked distance between the greatest biparietal width and the bifrontal line. This type is opposed to the *latus,* which is short.

6th. SPHEROID (*sphaeroides*).

The general character of this cranial form is the rounding of the frontal, parietal, parieto-occipital and the inferior or basal parts of the occiput itself, by spherical curves.

The cranium is relatively wide and short, the forehead and frontal large, the cranial arch widely convex, the occiput without protuberance, but rounding, the base wide (Fig. 13).

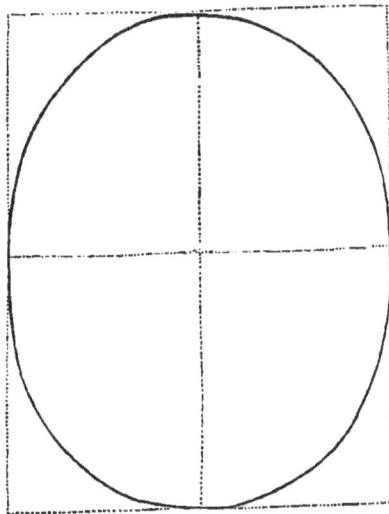

FIG. 13.—SPHAEROIDES.

I have already distinguished three principal forms of the spheroid, visible from the norma verticalis.

1st. *Sphaeroides* proper, which we also find subdivided.

2d. *Sphaerotocephalus,* which diverges by having a forehead wider but slightly retreating, following, therefore, the spheroidal as far as the coronal curve, and which as a whole becomes less even in its curves than the typical spheroid proper.

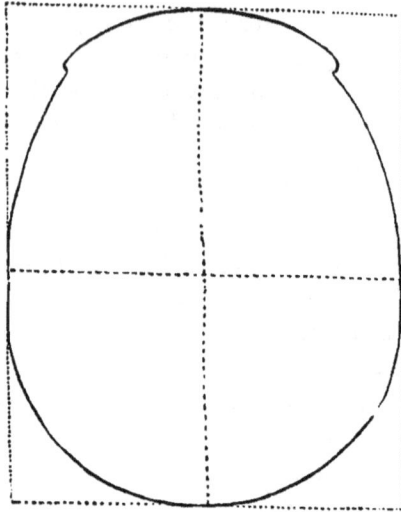

FIG. 14.—STRONGYLOCEPHALUS.

3d. *Strongylocephalus.* This type differs in that it has a narrowng in its sphenoidal fossae, visible in Fig. 14, so that the spherical part of the cranium is that which remains back of this narrowing.

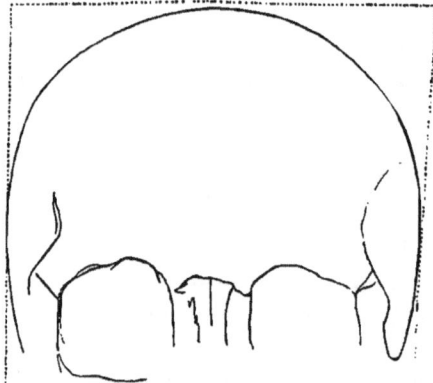

FIG. 15.—STRONGYLOCEPHALUS.

Fig. 15 shows also very well the frontal narrowing in its temporal lines, while the transversal curve is clearly spheroidal.

7th. BIRSOID (*byrsoïdes*) (Fig. 16).

The apparent form of this cranial type is an ovoid, which is removed from the usual form, because it has a rather large biparietal expansion, which does not terminate at the apex of the egg, but is rounded off; moreover, the curves, which are directed from the larger to the frontal expansion, are concave, with dilatation of the frontal line. Thus this form seems to be that of an elongated purse, the opening of which is found at the bifrontal line and the bottom at the expansion of the parietal curves, whence the name of *byrsoïdes* (like a purse).

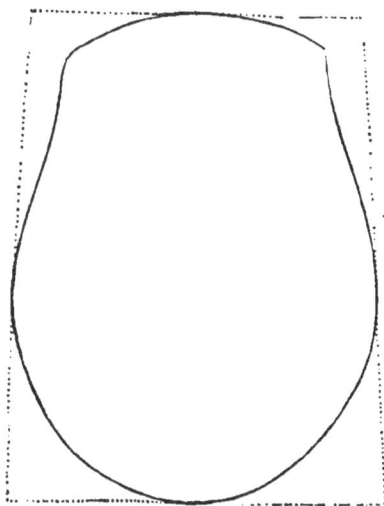

FIG. 16.—BYRSOIDES.

Observed from the side, the birsoid presents a superior plane; it is low, with the occipital rounding, but protuberant.

In its norma verticalis I have observed a variation among the birsoids of ancient Egypt; one with a smaller biparietal expansion. The cranium of this variety is large.

The seven forms which have been described are recognizable by the norma verticalis. The following are those in which the vertical is insufficient, uncertain or can be easily confounded with others which are different. Among these the following are found:

8th. PARALLELEPIPEDOID (*parallelepipedoides*).

Figures 17 and 19 represent a Sardinian type. The normal line has a slight swelling in the posterior part, and does not give the exact image of the form with parallel lines, while the lateral line corresponds to its name more closely. This form has a flat

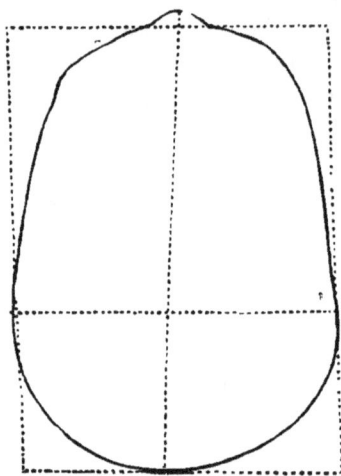

FIG. 17.—PARALLELEPIPEDOIDES SARDIN.

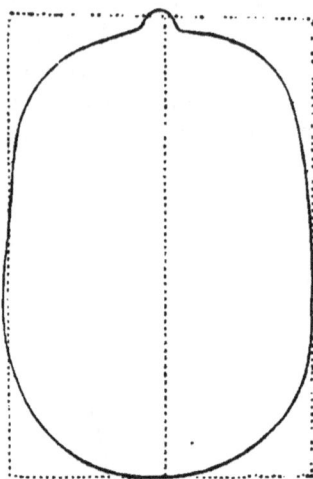

FIG. 18.—PARALLELEPIPEDOIDES KURGANICUS.

arch, vertical forehead, smooth occiput, and the base leveled; it is narrow, long, low, with smooth sides and evident corners, which makes a geometrical form.

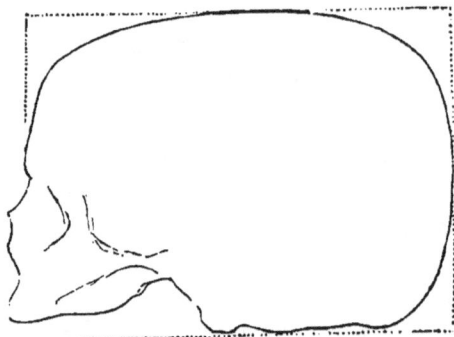

FIG. 19.—PARALLELEPIPEDOIDES SARDIN.

Figure 18 represents a *parallelepipedoid* from the Russian Kourgans. It appears very clear by the parallel lines of the two sides, its length and regularity.

This form is not very common, and can undergo variations in the norma verticalis, that is, can be larger in the transverse diameter, and hence relatively shorter; it is always low in the norma lateralis and through its entire length.

9th. CYLINDROID (*cylindroides*).

If the rounding of the corners and the sides of the parallelepipedoid renders it more convex, there is the " cylindroid," which is long, narrow, low, like the first, but rounded all around.   Therefore the forehead is lower, retreating (Fig. 20), and, seen from the vertical, the occiput is narrow (Fig. 21); this occurs in the types here given, of which one (Fig. 21) is from Latium, the other from the Russian Kourgans.   Such a form is rather rare, as is also the parallelepipedoid.

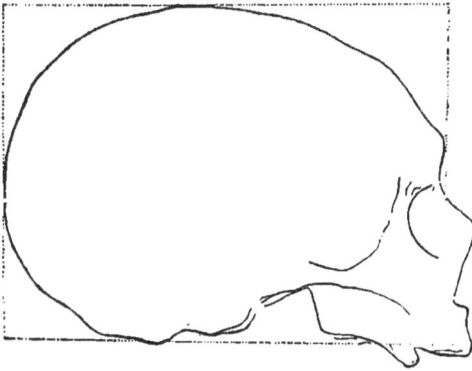

FIG. 20.—CYLINCROIDES.

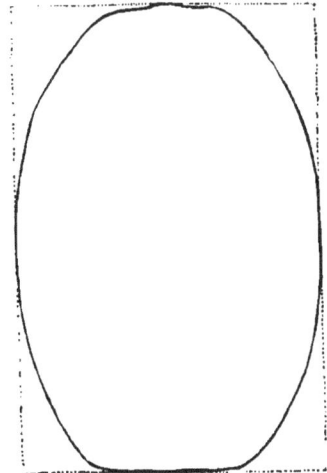

FIG. 21.—CYLINDROIDES.

10th. CUBOID (*cuboides*).

The cranium resembling a cube, has the arch, the occipital, and the sides smooth, and possibly the forehead, which is almost always vertical, at least in the small cuboids.   One cubical form, which approaches nearer to its typical name, has the vertical line about corresponding to a quadrilateral, a little elongated; but we know that the anterior is always narrower than the posterior part of the cranium.   As a rule, such a cranial form is more visible from the norma verticalis (Fig. 22) and from the posterior (Fig. 23).   The characteristic of the norma occipitalis is especially that the height is almost always equal to the width; hence we obtain the true cubical form from the side, this presenting a superficies of the cube.

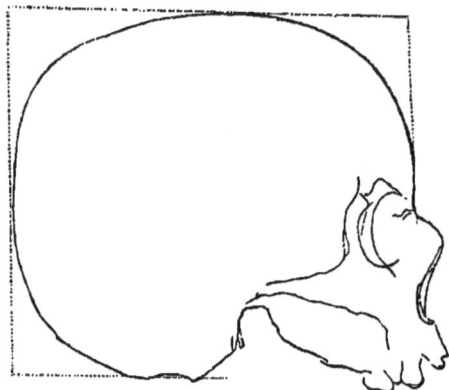

FIG. 22.—CUBOIDES PARVUS.   FIG. 23.—CUBOIDES PARVUS.

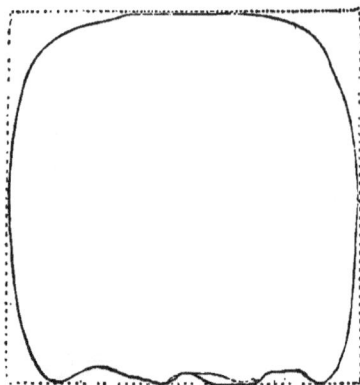

Figure 24 represents a *cuboides magnus* (from the Kourgans), while Figs. 22 and 23 reproduce a *cuboides parvus* of Sardinia.

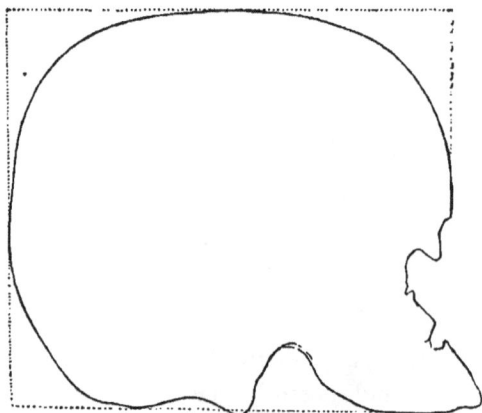

FIG. 24.—CUBOIDES MAGNUS.

Masculine cuboids may be found, especially large ones, with retreating foreheads and frontal sinuses large, and differing from the type Fig. 24.

The forms which follow are determined especially by the norma lateralis; first of all is the

11th. TRAPEZOID (*trapezoides*).

The two parallel sides of the trapezium here correspond to the

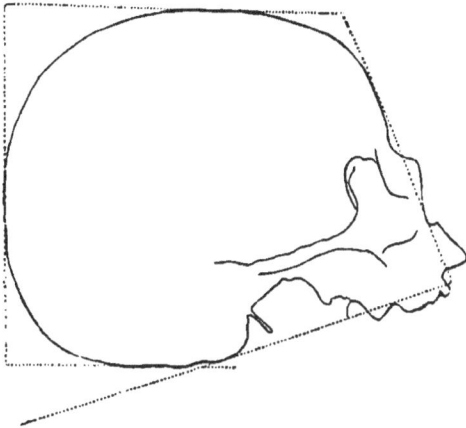

FIG. 25.—TRAPEZOIDES SARDINIENSIS.

arch and the base of the cranium (Fig. 25), the two sides not parallel are the sloping of the forehead, and the occiput more or

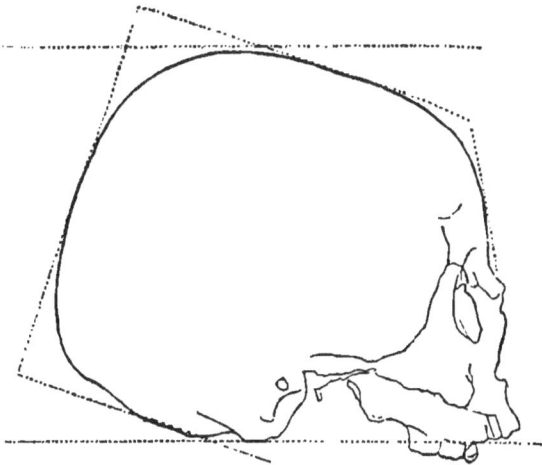

FIG. 26.—TRAPEZOIDES AFRICUS.

less oblique. The type which I show is the *trapezoides sardinien-sis*, a small microcephalous cranium. One important variation of the trapezoid is that which I have called African (*africus*),

which I have obtained from Harar, and which I have seen again in
Russia, especially in the Government of the Chersonesus.

The Sardinian type is distinguished by being higher in the
back, wider in the norma verticalis, and relatively short (Fig. 26).

In order to recognize this form it is necessary to know that the
greater height of the cranium is at the back, and thence there is
a perceptible sloping towards the forehead, which is low.   The

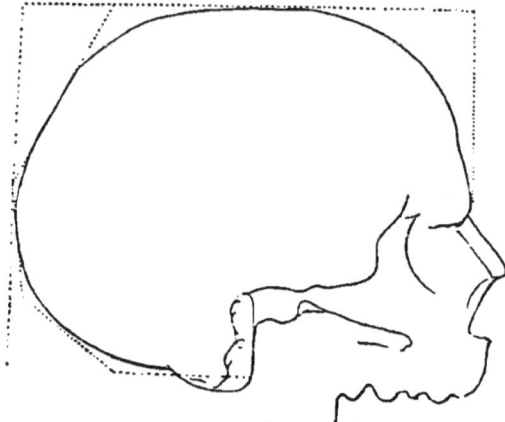

FIG. 27.—ACMONOIDES (TVER).

occipital is raised on an inclined plane, very sloping, while the base
of the cranium does not rest upon the same plane through its
entire length.

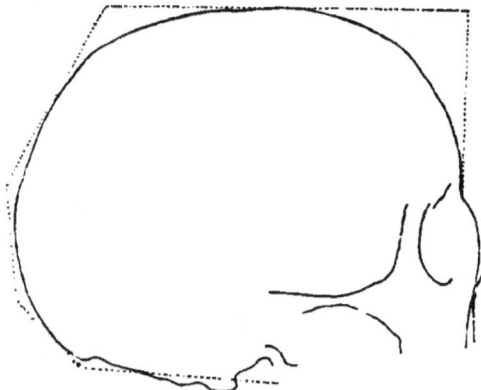

FIG. 28.—ACMONOIDES SICULUS.

12th. ACMONOID (*acmonoides*) (Figs. 27, 28).

It is not difficult to distinguish this variety with its anvil-like form.
Once seen, it becomes impressed on the memory by the singularity

of its shape. A long cranium, the norma verticalis not elliptical nor ovoid, because the sides are straight, a slight swelling of the parietal protuberances situated very far back, and the occipital resembling a quadrangular pyramid, leaning slightly on its cranial base. The cranium is high on the side, the forehead vertically inclined, but a little elevated; the arch is on the horizontal plane, abruptly inclined at the summit of the occipital pyramid, the extremity or protuberance of the occipital level. It has quite a large capacity. The types given here are derived (Fig. 27) from the Russian Kourgans, (Fig. 28) from modern Sicily.

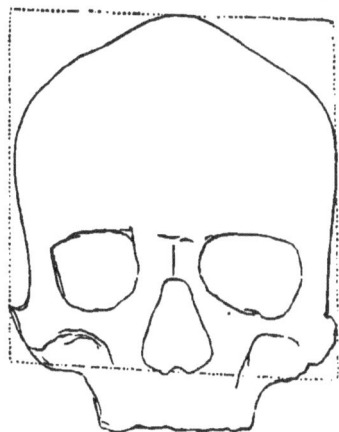

FIG. 29.—LOPHOCEPHALUS.   FIG. 30.—LOPHOCEPHALUS.

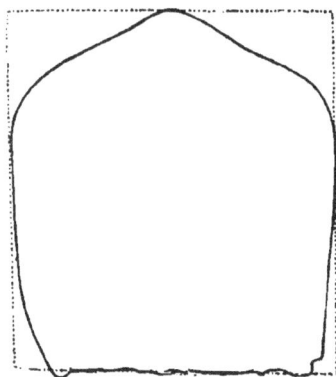

13th. LOPHOCEPHALIC (*lophocephalus*) (Figs. 29, 30).

This variety has a conspicuous trait not seen from the norma verticalis nor norma lateralis, but from the norma facialis and the norma occipitalis. This is, as shown in Figs. 29 and 30, the median eminence extending from the forehead to the sagittal. This eminence, which I call *lophus* (*lophos*), and which is described by other anthropologists as " crania with the arch of the backbone of an ass," or " arch like the keel of a ship," commences in the upper part of the frontal, at the place where the frontal curve first becomes horizontal. It is an elevation of the median portion, with lateral depressions amounting to a slight concavity, which reaches the coronal, the highest part of the eminence and surpasses it, invading the sagittal, where it terminates at the apex of the triangle, gradually disappearing.

This variety I have described among the crania of Melanesia, and the type which I give is from there; but it is not limited to that region and presents certain variations.

14th. CHOMATOCEPHALUS (*chomatocephalus*) (Fig. 31).

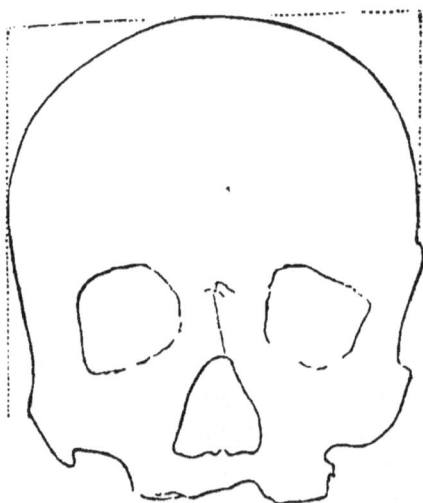

We call "tumulus-like" (*chomo*) that cranium which is elevated like a hill upon a horizontal plane passing through the orbital arches. It is not spherical, and slopes almost equally on all sides, starting at the summit of the cranial arch, which is much elevated, as seen in Fig. 31. Such a cranial arch may not always be regular in its inclinations, nor perfectly symmetrical, and not like a hill or gradual elevations of land, but should resemble a high elevation, and be almost disproportionate to the face. The type presented is from Melanesia. It is large, with a large capacity; there are also smaller and different types, both in the same region and elsewhere.

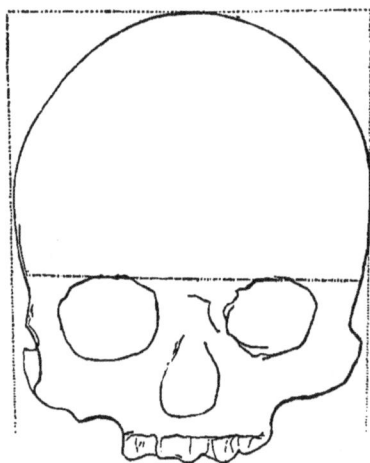

FIG. 31.—CHOMATOCEPHALUS.   FIG. 32.—PLATYCEPHALUS.

15th. PLATYCEPHALIC (*platycephalus*).

Platycephaly usually concerns the arch of the cranium only. It is flat, in a relative degree to the usual convexity. In fact it is a curve of the cranial arch which resembles an arc of a circle with a large radius; the platycephalic forms will be distinguishable in proportion as this idea is considered. As a rule the cranium is also wide in its transverse diameter, and hence it is also relatively short, as seen in the brachycephalic, Figs. 32, 33 and 34. Fig. 32, which is the profile of an Italian cranium, resembles strongly Fig. 33, which is a Russo-Kourgan; Fig. 34 is the norma verticalis of the latter and shows its relative width.

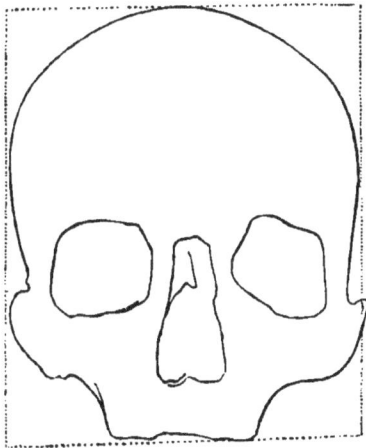

FIG. 33.—PLATYCEPH. BOGDANOVII.   FIG. 34.—PLATYCEPH. BOGDANOVII.

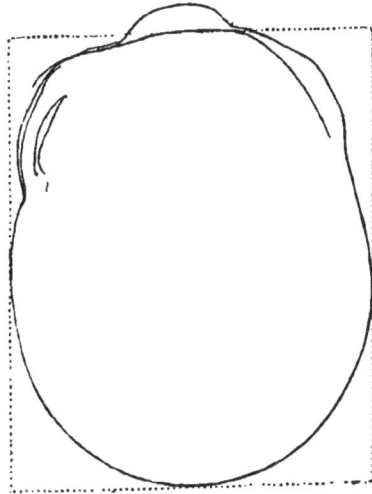

This characteristic is so evident and so much a part of the cranial form, to which a pathological signification has been erroneously attributed, that it alone is sufficient to constitute a distinct variety. It is easy to distinguish a cranium by such a characteristic without directly considering the norma facialis or norma occipitalis, and hence it is a good characteristic for classification. Among platycephalous forms there is one which is prominent on account of the unusual lowness of the arch, besides being very flat. It presents a small forehead and a general depression of the cranium from the orbital apophysis to the superior plane. The top of the cranium resembles a flat cake or a bun, whence the name *placuntoides* which I have given to it, that is, the form of a flat cake (Fig. 35). There are also platycephali with narrow foreheads, which I will consider later.

16th. SKOPELOID (*skopeloides*) (Fig. 36).

The form which I call "rock-like" (*skopelos*) is very curious. It has a summit on the posterior part of the cranium which slopes from every side, and at the occiput descends rapidly to the base. The cranium is large, wide at the base, with a narrow forehead, and the frontal slightly sloping, following the inclined plane of the posterior summit.

FIG. 35.—PLACUNTOIDES.

This form is difficult to describe, and Fig. 36 gives an imperfect idea of it.

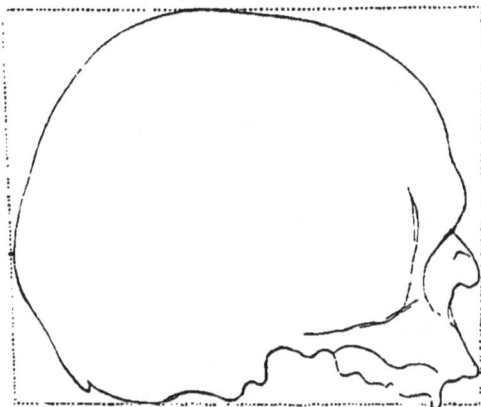

FIG. 36.—SKOPELOIDES SAMNITICUS.

Of this variety, so characteristic and quite common in Samos, I have seen some which are microcephalous, in Samos and likewise in the Russian Kourgans, although there very rare.

The sixteen human varieties above described I have determined, after observations of more than 3500 crania, principally
from the Mediterranean, prehistoric tombs, and modern Russia,
the crania of the Kourgans, and from some ancient cemeteries in
Moscow and the Chersonesus, and from Melanesia, I can affirm
nothing of the entire number of human varieties, nor of their distribution, before making new and direct personal observations in
the rest of Europe and in other parts of the world; I wait in confi-
dence and with the earnest desire of making such observations.
I affirm with some personal satisfaction that, as regards the new
anthropological method, I have surmounted its uncertainties.
The number of varieties has been much reduced, and they are
separated by definite and recognizable characteristics.

I cannot affirm that new varieties may not be found even in the
Mediterranean field, where I have chiefly extended my researches.
If they should be found they would be few, and probably brought
from other localities.

II.

Subvarieties.

Though the number of varieties which I have until now determined in the Mediterranean and Russia, together with some from
Melanesia, is limited to sixteen only, the subvarieties are much
more numerous. Subvarieties should first of all preserve the
characteristics of the variety of which they are a variation, and
should have some other characteristic, which must not be transitory and individual, but fixed and hereditary. Groups of subvarieties must constitute real groups; the variety is the principal
denomination of characteristics common to many subvarieties,
which add to the primary or dominant characteristic one or several
new characteristics which separate the subvarieties from each
other, as the following scheme exhibits:

Variety: A.

Subvariety: A + a, A + b, A + c, A + d, and so on.

While the characteristic A gives the name to the variety, the
less general characteristics a, b, c, d give the subvarieties of A.

The same relation is found in the animal kingdom between genera and species, or between species and varieties; in the first place, the universal characteristics of the genus are limited by those of the species; in the second, those of the species are restricted by those of the varieties, and those of the variety by the subvarieties. I have above stated that while in my opinion the name of variety is general in its meaning, and therefore also provisional, it may remain definitive by further study and assume a fixed signification. Different results may be reached, but the classification will remain unaltered, because the characteristics will continue stable and the method unchanged.

In determining the characteristics of numerous series of crania, and in arranging groups of one variety, another plan occurred to me, that of finding characteristics which separate a subvariety into groups of a third order, meaning by a group of the 1st order the variety; then we shall have a plan like the following:

1st. Variety: A.

2d. Subvariety : $A + a$, $A + b$, $A + c$, etc.

3d. Sub-subvariety : $A + a + \alpha$, $A + a + \beta$, $A + a + \gamma$.

The characteristics α, β, γ are not transitory; they are stable, and, on this account, of the same type as those which distinguish the subvarieties a, b, c, etc.

It is easy to answer an inquiry as to the manner of distinguishing these characteristics: individual variations are not repeated, and they therefore do not occur in many individuals, unless accidentally; not only do they cause little divergence from the typical forms, they constitute oscillations of the same form recognizable as such. It is not so with the characteristics of subgroups of the 2d or 3d order; they alter the fundamental form in some part, and are repeated in groups composed of several individual elements.

We have seen how we may determine varieties, which in a great measure assume geometrical forms and receive corresponding names, because of their approximation to bodies with well-known geometrical characters. We have also seen that we can determine the form of this irregular body, the brain, either by the vertical or lateral norm, or in some cases by the anterior or posterior aspect. Besides the normae which determine the variety, there remain other normae which have various characters, and can therefore complete the craniological type or show its variations beyond the primary character which places it in a given variety. An ellipsoid, regarded vertically, may have different normae laterales, at the same time remaining an ellipsoid; it may also have other characteristics, visible from the norma occipitalis, which make it vary from another cranium, also ellipsoid, with a different norma occipitalis. There may also be variation in the same norma which gives the fundamental form; for example, the ellipsoid (Fig. 38) is shorter and relatively wider than the one beside it (Fig. 37),

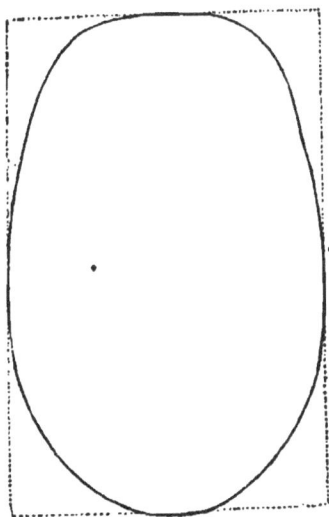

FIG. 37.—DOLICHELLIPSOIDES.　　　FIG. 38.—BRACHYELLIPSOIDES.

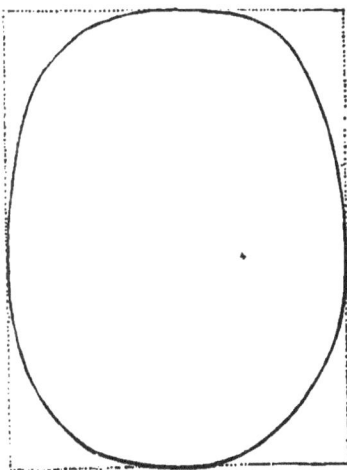

which is therefore a " dolichellipsoid," while those wide and short, like Fig. 38, we may call " brachyellipsoids." Such variations of elliptical forms correspond to the structure of the cranium, and therefore constitute subvarieties.

Following the order above carried out in the varieties, I commence with the ellipsoid.

I. ELLIPSOIDES.

1st. *Ellips. depressus.*

This is visible from the norma lateralis and also from the norma anterior (Fig. 39). Cranium low from the vertex to the occipital base, as if crushed in every direction from the frontal and lateral sides, and therefore with a narrow, retreating forehead, of curved form; the same of the occiput. This curious and characteristic form is subject to variations which would take too long to describe here.

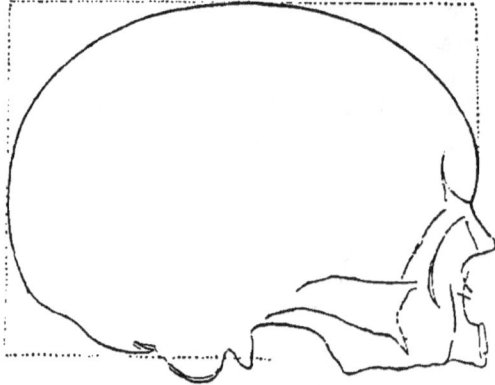

FIG. 39.—ELLIPS. DEPRESSUS.

2d. *Ellips. isopericampylus* (Fig. 40).

Isopericampylus signifies "with equal curves all around"; the character of this subvariety is especially that the form is handsome and perfect. It may have variations in the form of the ellipse and in some other characters.

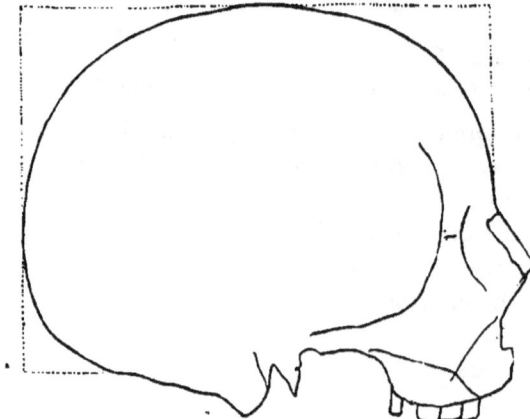

FIG. 40.—ELLIPS. ISOPERICAMPYLUS.

3d. *Ellips. embolicus.*

From *embolus*, prow, because the occipital decline, which commences well forward, reaches as far as the cranial base, and such a projection has the apparent form of a ship's prow. I at first called this form *emboloïdes meridionalis*, because I had observed it among the crania of Southern Italy. I found it again in Russia

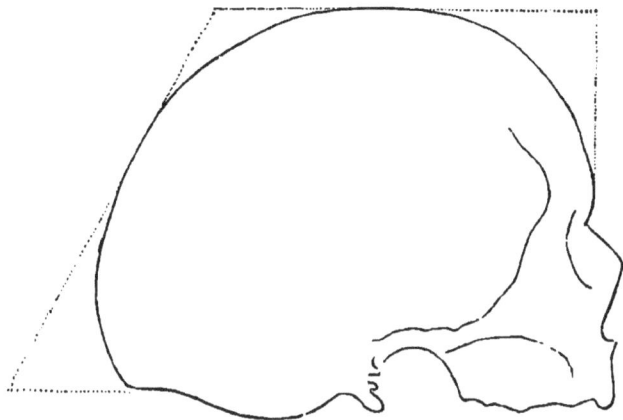

FIG. 41.—ELLIPS. EMBOLICUS.

among the Kourgan crania, among Etruscan crania, ancient Roman, and finally at Novilara (Pesaro) in tombs perhaps of the

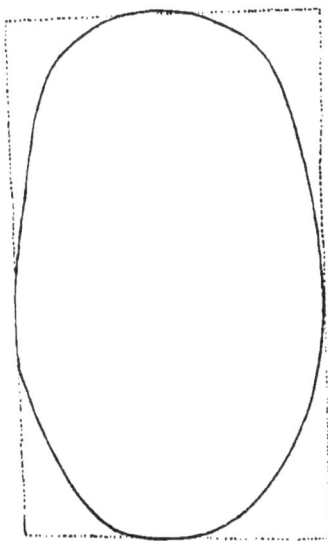

FIG. 42.—STENELLIPS. EMBOLICUS.

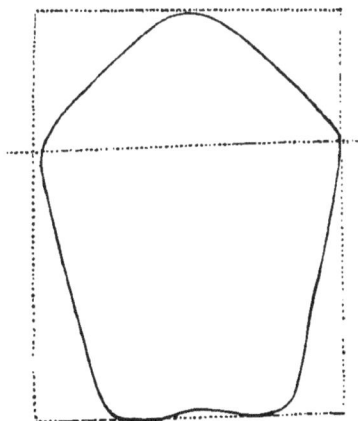

FIG. 43.—STENELLIPS. HYPSISTEGOIDES.

5th century before the Christian era. Fig. 41 is the profile of a cranium of the Kourgans of Tver. This cranium, that is, this cranial form with definite ellipses, is long and at times exceeds 200 mm., and differs in width.   In the meridional emboloid it is 135-138 mm., but in others is below 130 mm.; hence the name of *stenellipsoides embolicus* which I have given it, as in the cranium from Novilara which I have shown here (Fig. 42).

4th. *Ellips. hypsistegoides* (Fig. 43).

This form is visible from the posterior norma of the cranium, as in Fig. 43 (cranium from Novilara).   The arch is constructed like a roof in the example here given, and the height of the cranium from the base to the vertex is considerable.   There are *stegoid* varieties also, that is, with a roof-like arch, not very high.

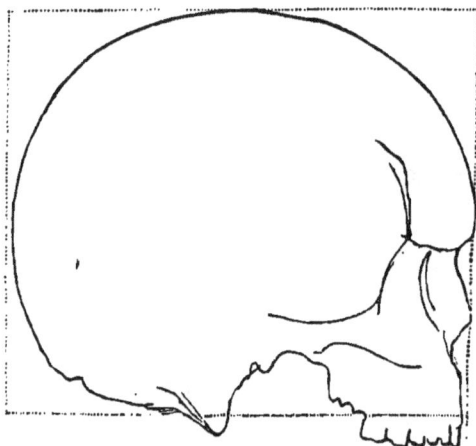

FIG. 44.—ELLIPS. CORYTHOCEPHALUS.

5th. *Ellips. corythocephalus* (Fig. 44).

" Helmet-like cranium," high, with a fine curve from the forehead to the occiput as far as the base, of large capacity, and flat at the sides.   This gives it the appearance of a helmet.   I found it first among ancient Egyptian crania, whence its name of *aegyptiacus ;* then among the Kourgan crania.

6th. *Ellips. epiopisthius.*   That is, a cranium of elliptical form in which the level rises from the frontal towards the posterior part, so that the latter appears to be raised (Fig. 45).

7th. *Ellips. scalenus.* The *epiopisthius* can also be, as in this case, *scalenus*, a rapid obliquity from the occipital slope. But the *cranio-scalenus* can also be found without being *epiopisthius*, and

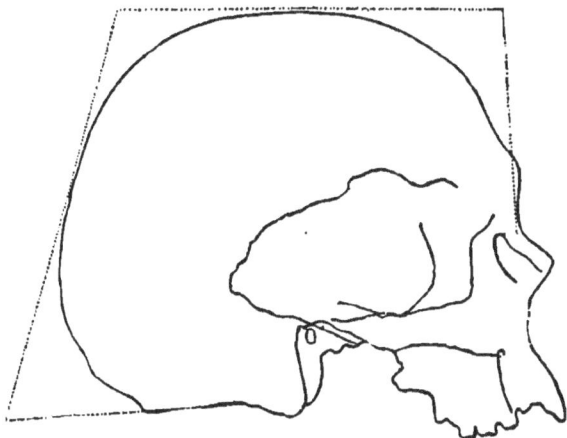

FIG. 45.—ELLIPS. EPIOPISTHIUS.

vice versa. These two characteristics appear separately and together in other varieties, as in the ovoid, the platycephalus, and in the ellipsoidal subvariety. This may also be said of the roof-like form, or *stegoid*, and of the *hypsistegoid*.

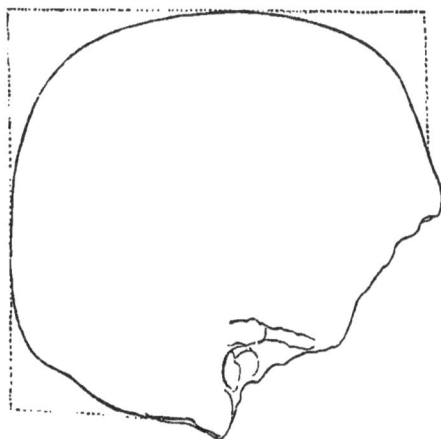

FIG. 46.—ELLIPS. TETRAGONALIS.

8th. *Ellips. tetragonalis* (Fig. 46).

This ellipsoidal form is very characteristic in its norma lateralis, which has the appearance of a tetragon, whence its name. The cranium is high, the forehead as a rule erect, the occiput perpendicular and very convex and depressed at the sides. It may be confused with the cuboid when seen only from the norma lateralis. But I must now omit a series of subgroups and limit myself to the principal forms.

II. *Pentagonoides.*—With regard to varieties, I have distinguished various pentagonoids, *acutus, obtusus, oblongus, brachypentagonoides ;* and there may be *stegoids, cristati,* etc.

III. *Rhomboides.*—The rhomboids are also short, *brachyrhomboides,* or elongated in the anterior part, *oblongus.*

IV. *Ovoides.*—Subvarieties of ovoids are found with wedge-like occiput, *cuneatus, scalenus, stegoides, depressus.*

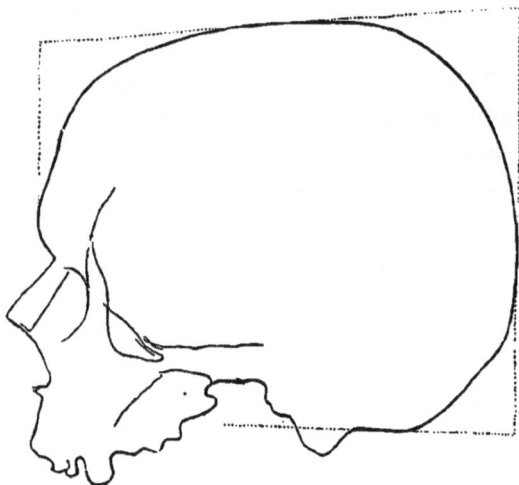

FIG. 47.—SPHEN. TETRAGONUS.

V. *Sphenoides.*—By the norma verticalis I have distinguished *sphenoides, stenometopus, sph. rotundus, spelatus, sph. megas, sph. oblongus ;* an important subvariety is found in *tetragonus* (Fig. 47), which is not only sphenoidal in the vertical, but also in the lateral, and has prominent corners, rendering the vertex and sides plane.

There is likewise a sphenoid, *cyrtocephalus,* which has a convexity extending from the frontal and parietals to the vertex, resembling a protuberance, though not so pronounced as to constitute a *crista* or a *lophos ;* if these two characteristics are found, the *sph.* is *cristatus* or *lophoides* (Fig. 48).

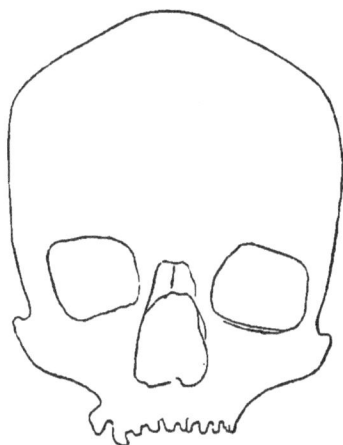

FIG. 48.—SPHEN. CRISTATUS.

VI. *Sphaeroides.*—I have given the principal variations of this variety, that is :

a) *sphaerotocephalus ;*
b) *sphaeroides, hemisphaeroides ;*
c) *strongylocephalus* (see above).

VII. *Byrsoides.*—So far I have only found one variation from the *siculus,* that is, the *aegyptiacus,* which is a little narrower (see above).

VIII., IX., X. *Parallelepipedoides, Cylindroides, Cuboides* (see varieties).

XI. *Trapezoides.*—I have already distinguished two subvarieties with the names of *Trap. sardiniensis* and *Trap. africus.* These are the most typical and commonest variations; in my catalogue of Russian varieties several other secondary forms are found, of which the commonest is *trap. rotundatus.*

There is a subvariety which I considered during my first observations as a distinct variety, and which I had named *Pyrgoides,* a cranium resembling the form of a tower. This cranium is also a trapezoid, but it is larger, the occiput is high and perpendicular, so that the vertex of the cranium coincides very far back with the bregma. It is large enough to appear spheroid, the anteposterior declivity slopes uniformly from the back.

I preserve the name *Pyrgoides* for such forms because the occipital looks like the wall of a tower, high and quadrangular; but I consider it a subvariety of the trapezoid. I have noticed variations in *Pyrg. romanus.* The type in Fig. 49 is a *cyrtocephalus,* so called on account of the fronto-bregmatic protuberance, a *rotundatus* on account of the truncated corners and the convex faces.

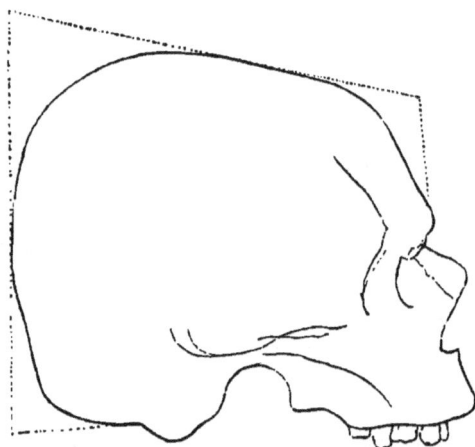

FIG. 49.—PYRGOIDES.

XII. *Acmonoides.*—Of this singular variety I have found subvarieties: a) *siculus,* which is the typical form described; b) *megalometopus,* or having a large, wide forehead; c) *obtusus,* on account of the rounded corners; d) *stegoides,* on account of the roof-like arch; e) *subtilis,* because narrower than the type; f) *proophyrocus,* because it has prominent frontal sinuses which do not exist in the type.

XIII. *Lophicephalus.*—This variety offers some variations from the type from Melanesia before presented; its principal characteristic does not consist in the *lophos,* but in the cranial form being a little larger. It is found among the Kourgans (Fig. 50); the width is greater posteriorly, and the lateral parts more convex, *loph. kurganicus.*

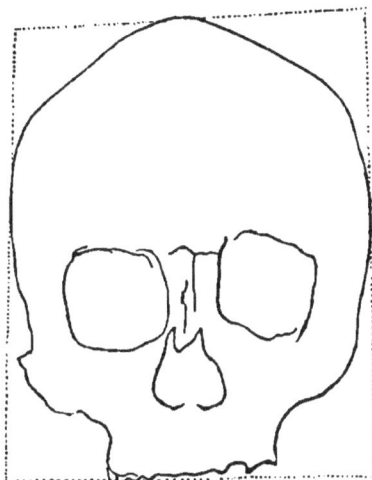

FIG. 50.—LOPHOC. KURGANICUS.

XIV. *Chomatocephalus.*

I have found subgroups with the following characteristics :

a) *Chom. angulosus,* because it has a surface with angular projections.

b) *Chom. summus,* on account of its great height.

c) *Chom. cristatus,* on account of its crest-like summit.

d) *Chom. sphenoidalis,* for its wedge-like form as observed from the norma verticalis.

XV. *Platycephalus.*—The varieties with ˙most subvarieties are the *Ellipsoides,* the *Sphenoides,* and the *Platycephalus.* Of the *Platyc.* I have so far been able to distinguish 22 varieties, of which several also have subgroups, as the *Isobathyplatycephalus,* which I have called *siculus* because first found in the tombs of the neolithic age in Sicily (Fig. 51). We find:

a) *Platyc. cuneatus ;* b) *platyc. humilus ;* c) *stenometopus ;* d) *platyc. brachymetopus ;* e) *euryplatymetopus ;* f) *platyc. embolicus ;* g) *platyc. rotundus ;* h) *platyc. scalenus,* and so on.

XVI. *Scopeloides.*—A common form in *Samos*, and should be more sought after in Italy.

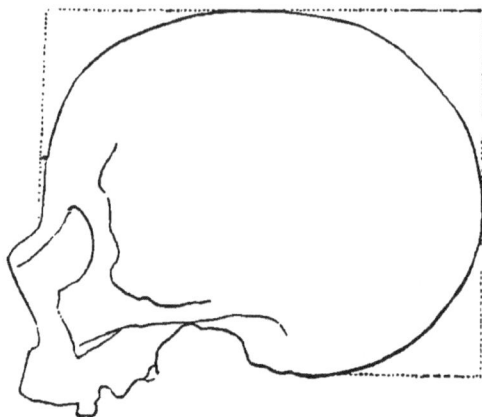

FIG. 51.—ISOBATHYPLATYC. SICULUS.

In ending this description of subvarieties, at present limited to those of the sixteen human varieties (and which I consider incomplete in number, just as I have considered incomplete the number of varieties of the Mediterranean and Kourgans of Russia, where I have found the varieties described), I should add, in order to complete the picture of subvarieties, another characteristic of classification, of which I have above spoken, the volume of the cranium.

As I have said, what is well known in regard to other animals occurs in man, that large and small varieties are found, both in stature and in the volume of the cranium, and these differences in size and volume are not indications of functional superiority or of priority. The functions of the brain of 1200 gr. can be just as perfect as those of a brain of 1600 gr., and it is known that not all large and voluminous brains are those of great men, nor are those of inferior or commonplace human types small. I have found ellipsoids, cuboids, ovoids, pentagonoids, platycephali, trapezoids, large, medium, and small, with complete and perfect structures in the large as well as in the small and microcephalic varieties; for this reason I have thought it wise to consider types of different volume or cranial capacity as subvarieties, and not to confuse the capacity of one with another.

I have also found that certain cranial types have a special capacity which does not belong to another type. Thus the trapezoids have a small capacity, between elatto- and microcephalic, and never exceed that limit; that of the pyrgoids is greater; the stenocephali have a small capacity; the coritocephali are megalocephalic, and so on.

I have adopted the words *megas, magnus, maximus* for the large and largest varieties, *medius* for the medium, and *parvus* and *micros* for the small and smallest varieties. In respect to the capacity when measured, we may practically consider *micros* as far as the average of 1150 cc.; *parvus*, as far as the average 1350 cc. ; *megas*, from 1500 up ; *maximus*, beyond 1700 cc. Thus the number of subvarieties becomes increased.

III.

Nomenclature.

Nomenclature is necessary in the classification of animals, of plants and minerals. Names aid to discern forms, to recognize general characteristics by means of which series and groups are formed, to distinguish series from each other. Without names we should not know of what we speak. Thus in the classification of human varieties and subvarieties it is necessary to adopt technical names in order to indicate them; although we may but imperfectly express the entire conception of the form which we wish to indicate.

For this purpose I have selected words from the Greek and secondarily from the Latin languages, because Greek words are better adapted for proper names, and are easily constructed, while words in use in a modern language would be difficult to foreigners, and having a vulgar signification, would be equivocal; finally, because many languages derive names of geometrical forms from Greek and Latin, and hence such can easily be understood.

It may appear that I have too much increased the number of technical names in my earlier memoir, *Human Varieties of Melanesia.* In a measure that is true, but most of the words for each variety were in use previously. *Brachy, meso, dolichocephalo, hypsi, chamecephalo, lepto, chameprosopo, lepto, meso, platyrinno, brachy, leptostafilino* and the like are not my words. It appeared that the vocabulary would be enormous and sibylline when other expressions were added to the name of *stenocephalo,* etc. The French school, as regards nomenclature, is the most exaggerated. I need but state that besides the words above given and common to all anthropological schools, it has *basion, episthion, pterion, obelion, inion, nasion, ophryon, metopion, stphanion* and the like. If in adopting the zoological method which I have indicated we abandon craniometry, and with it its nomenclature, there will remain but few technical terms for the indications of varieties and subvarieties, and then nomenclature will be brief and significative. Whoever reads my Memoirs from the first, that upon the Melanesians, to the last, upon " microcephalic varieties," will observe how I have little by little eliminated names and confusing and wearisome measurements, and have reduced classification by technical terms for nomenclature to the greatest simplicity.

Objections made against the nomenclature which I have introduced can also be applied to that used in zoology and botany and in all the sciences which have one. An important objection seems to me that of Professor Benedict of Vienna, who would like to abolish every word of Greek and Latin origin, because they are dead languages which in a few years will no longer be taught in schools of science. I agree with him. But, as I have above said, it matters little whether a technical name of a variety be understood in its signification provided that the variety denominated be known by means of the name, and nothing more, when it refers to a determinate form. Moreover, a reform in classification should not suffer through a difficulty in names, which, if they were Italian, would not be easily accepted and understood by strangers. Greek and Latin have at least the advantage of being languages which can now be universally retained for the sciences. The objections, or rather I should say the observations, made by Hovelacque and Mantegazza are of no value and do not merit attention.

I at first adopted technical names Italianized, but afterwards, in order to render the meaning easy to foreigners, I adopted the Latinized form, which has the advantage of preserving the original vowels and consonants. The naturalist, accustomed to zoological nomenclature, finds nothing new, much less strange, in this method, and the anthropologist is a naturalist who is occupied exclusively with man.

I consider it useful and opportune to prepare catalogues of the varieties and subvarieties, and to record the geographical distribution of forms; they are pictures which render two facts evident, the number of ethnic elements and their dispersion.

I hope by this method and by these principles a systematic anthropology may be constituted, which may be the foundation for scientific researches upon the origin of human races, upon their number and distribution, upon their crossings, and, finally, upon the possible solution of the problems of the unity or plurality of the species.